REAL-WORLD PROJECTS

How do I design relevant and engaging learning experiences?

SUZIE
BOSS

ASCD Alexandria, VA USA

ASCD | arias™

Website: www.ascd.org   www.ascdarias.org
E-mail: books@ascd.org

Printed in the United States of America. Cover art © 2015 by ASCD. ASCD publications present a variety of viewpoints. The views expressed or implied in this book should not be interpreted as official positions of the Association.

ASCD LEARN TEACH LEAD® and ASCD ARIAS™ are trademarks owned by ASCD and may not be used without permission. All other referenced trademarks are the property of their respective owners.

PAPERBACK ISBN: 978-1-4166-2029-7   ASCD product #SF115043
Also available as an e-book (see Books in Print for the ISBNs).

Library of Congress Cataloging-in-Publication Data
Boss, Suzie.
  Real-world projects : how do I design relevant and engaging learning experiences? / Suzie Boss.
     pages cm
  Includes bibliographical references and index.
  ISBN 978-1-4166-2029-7 (pbk. : alk. paper) 1. Project method in teaching. I. Title.
  LB1027.43.B66 2015
  371.3'6--dc23
                              2014045105

21 20 19 18 17 16 15   1 2 3 4 5 6 7 8 9 10 11 12 13 14

REAL-WORLD PROJECTS

How do I design relevant and engaging learning experiences?

Want to earn a free ASCD Arias e-book?
Your opinion counts! Please take 2–3 minutes to give
us your feedback on this publication. All survey
respondents will be entered into a drawing to
win an ASCD Arias e-book.

Please visit
www.ascd.org/ariasfeedback

Thank you!

Introduction to Project-Based Learning

Like many schools, Sonora Elementary in Springdale, Arkansas, has a vision of preparing today's students to become tomorrow's leaders. This is more than a catchy slogan on a web page: teachers and school leaders regularly encourage Sonora students to take the lead on solving problems that matter to them.

What does this look like in action? Picture two 4th grade girls who want to share their love of reading and improve their school's literacy rate. They start to formulate an action plan to get books into the hands of classmates during the summer. Because their school integrates technology across the curriculum, these girls are adept at using tools that enable them to map and analyze data. When they map the addresses of all 700 of the school's students, they notice a high concentration of children in neighborhoods with apartment complexes. That information helps them plan a route and schedule for a mobile library. They even customize the recommended book selections to match students' reading levels and interests. When the girls present their well-crafted proposal for a mobile library to a local car dealer, he's sold. He donates a van to put their summer reading plan into action (Miller, Vaughan, & Worthy, 2014).

When students are engaged in real-world problem solving, they're in the driver's seat of their own learning. They don't ask that tired question, "When will we ever need to know this?" They're motivated to develop new skills and master challenging content because they recognize the usefulness of what they're learning.

Real-world learning makes education more relevant and purposeful. Through such experiences, students learn to recognize problems worth solving and get good at communicating their thinking. What's more, they develop a sense of agency. This powerful idea—that young people are capable of taking action and making things happen—puts students on the path to active citizenship.

Why This Focus?

The strategies in this book have emerged from more than a decade of interviews, classroom observations, and professional development related to project-based learning, or PBL. Through my work with teachers and students in diverse settings, both in the United States and internationally, I've seen a wide range of projects that emphasize real-world connections while addressing rigorous learning goals. For example, middle school students learn about geography and finance by using microlending to support entrepreneurs in the developing world. High school students apply their communication skills and critical thinking to convince their classmates not to become dropout statistics. Elementary school students gain an understanding of habitats by teaming up with ranchers and farmers on conservation projects.

Although teachers often tell me they can see why real-world projects would engage their students, many are uncertain of how to design and manage projects that involve issues, experts, and audiences beyond their classrooms.

In this brief publication, you will find practical strategies for identifying project-worthy ideas, connecting with experts and allies, and thinking critically about the role of authentic audiences. Project examples are woven throughout, showing what real-world learning looks like in action. Resources in the Encore section will help you plan your next steps.

Here's some good news: designing real-world learning experiences doesn't require an extensive technology infrastructure or heavy investment in professional development. It does take teachers who are willing to consider how content standards relate to the world beyond the classroom. School leaders play an important role by supporting teacher innovation in project design. It also helps to have a school culture that values student voice and parents who are supportive of learning experiences that may look quite different from what they remember of school. Connections to experts are important, too, for supporting students' efforts.

When those elements align, powerful learning results. Danette McMillian offers a good example. She teaches economics and civics at Maplewood High School in Nashville, Tennessee. Many of her students have limited experiences outside their immediate neighborhood. That's why this teacher keeps her eyes open for projects that address academic goals, expand students' horizons, *and* enable them to improve their community. Sometimes students wind up improving their own lives in the process.

McMillian doesn't need to look far for inspiration. The street where the high school is located has no sidewalks. "It's dangerous for pedestrians. I've almost hit two students myself," she admits. To learn about the processes of government, students advocated for a sidewalk in front of their school. The project focus aligned perfectly with academic content: "This class is about how government works. How, as a citizen, do you get things to change?" McMillian says. She wants her students to not only understand how their government works, from the local to the national level, but also be able to apply what they know. "Then it means something to them. It's real-world. They can look back and say, 'This project helped me with my life'" (personal communication, August 22, 2014).

How can you create more opportunities to bring the world into your classroom, and bring your students into the world? Let's dig in. And in the following pages, watch for "think about it" prompts to connect what you are reading with what you notice in your own learning environment.

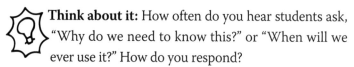 **Think about it:** How often do you hear students ask, "Why do we need to know this?" or "When will we ever use it?" How do you respond?

Building on the PBL Framework

Fortunately, you don't need to invent a brand-new instructional approach to connect students with the real world. Project-based learning offers a ready framework that deliberately emphasizes engagement, invites curiosity, and values student voice and choice.

As PBL has taken hold in a variety of contexts, different "flavors" of this instructional approach have emerged. Projects may last for a couple of weeks or an entire semester; they might focus on a single content area or take an interdisciplinary approach. Some teachers design their entire curriculum through PBL; others alternate projects with more traditional instruction.

Regardless of differences in implementation, PBL is always about learning by doing. Students learn deeply by asking and investigating questions, applying what they learn, and sharing their results with others. By working collaboratively, solving problems, and communicating their findings, students master more than content: they gain important knowledge, skills, and dispositions that prepare them for taking an active role in their 21st century world.

For these benefits to accrue, projects can't be treated as add-ons to the curriculum. PBL is about "main course" learning, not dessert (Larmer & Mergendoller, 2010). Because PBL puts an emphasis on students applying what they learn, this approach aligns with the expectations of the Common Core State Standards. Across grade levels, the standards call on students to think critically, solve problems creatively, and make well-reasoned arguments supported by evidence. These are all embedded in well-designed PBL. The same holds true for the Next Generation Science Standards and technology integration standards, such as the ISTE Standards for Students.

Leah Penniman (2014) is a science teacher who regularly engages her high school students in real-world projects. She explains how PBL fits squarely with an emphasis on academic standards:

> We can and should implement projects that simultaneously engage students in rigorous scientific thinking and provide opportunities for students to make tangible contributions to their communities. At Tech Valley High School in New York, science students are engaged in projects such as urban soil remediation, invasive species tracking, sensor engineering for water quality monitoring, mapping food deserts, and quantifying carbon sinks. They master content better because they are applying their learning to initiatives that truly matter. (para. 2)

The challenge is to design projects that don't just mimic real life but also enable students to engage directly with their world. Penniman (2014) explains why this is a choice worth making:

As educators, we have a choice about how to approach each curricular topic. When confronted with a mandate to ensure our students' understanding of the human immune system, we can reject a rote approach and instead hold a health fair for younger students in the district. If the topic is ecosystems, we can work with the Department of Environmental Conservation to monitor the ecology of a local park. When studying climate change, we can write to members of Congress to encourage science-based policies. By engaging in conversations with other educators and community leaders, we soon see that meaningful applications are abundant. (para. 8)

Before we explore strategies to put such meaningful projects into action, let's take a closer look at why real-world learning is worth the effort.

Giving Students a Reason to Engage

Learning experiences that challenge students to address authentic problems give them a reason to engage. Research about project-based learning shows that this approach heightens students' motivation to learn and their engagement (Thomas, 2000).

Why does this matter? The annual Gallup Student Poll (2013) points to the disturbing trend that students become less engaged the longer they stay in school. Only 55 percent of students in grades 5–12 report feeling engaged in school. Another 28 percent say they aren't engaged, while 17 percent are *actively* disengaged. Creativity, too, drops steadily from kindergarten through high school, according to global education expert Yong Zhao (2012).

These trends have long-term implications. In worst-case scenarios, students lose interest in school altogether. Although U.S. high school graduation rates are improving, schools continue to lose too many students, including a disproportionate number of Hispanic and African American youth, before graduation. Without a high school diploma, young people face a lifetime of diminished opportunities, from lower wages to shortened life expectancy (Amos, 2008). The segment of the population that is the least well educated is also the fastest growing. For many of these young people, the decision to drop out starts long before they reach their senior year.

In less dramatic ways, student engagement affects everything from classroom behavior to habits of mind. As Klem and Connell (2004) report, "Researchers have found student engagement a robust predictor of student achievement and behavior in school, regardless of socioeconomic status" (p. 262).

John Hattie (2012), drawing on meta-analysis of some 800 studies, describes an effective school climate as "one in which 'learning is cool,' worth engaging in, and everyone—teacher and students—is involved in the process of learning" (p. 29). In contrast, disengaged students "found their schoolwork uninteresting, were inclined to give up on challenging tasks, looked for distractions, failed to prepare for lessons, and opted out of class activities. These ambivalent students should be a focus of teachers' attention—and are perhaps the easiest to win back" (p. 126).

Persistent learners are willing to try new approaches when things don't go smoothly on the first try. They learn from what doesn't work, turning failure into a stepping-stone to success. These are essential habits of mind for problem solving, and critical for success in a fast-changing world filled with new challenges in need of solutions (Costa & Kallick, 2008). These mental habits won't develop in the absence of engagement. On the other hand, when students are invested in learning, you may find them exceeding expectations.

Elementary school teacher Jim Bentley from Elk Grove, California, has found that his students will read well above their comprehension level if the material relates to an issue they care about. In a project about government and citizenship, students lobbied for an exercise track around their campus to promote community fitness. Even with supporting health data, allies in the school and community, and a video they produced to support their cause, they ran into a roadblock when it came to budget approval. To advocate for a change in how construction funds would be allocated, students had to wade through densely written public policies and grasp complex budgeting processes. "I remember warning them, this is going to be hard. You're going to have to read material that wasn't intended for 6th graders," Bentley recalls (personal communication, July 15, 2014). Nevertheless, his students persisted and eventually were successful with their campaign.

Teacher Laurette Rogers saw similar results with her 4th grade science students, who wanted to take action to help save an endangered species. They focused on improving habitat for the California freshwater shrimp, a species native to the wetlands in their rural community. In a documentary about the project (*A Simple Question: The Story of STRAW* [White & Donnenfield, 2009]), Rogers explained how she and her students wrestled with unfamiliar scientific vocabulary en route to understanding the issues. In one scene, she recalls how she and her students "went through the scientific papers very slowly, as you can imagine, and learned about the species. We looked up words like *extirpated*—I didn't know what *extirpated* meant, either." Students (and teacher) were motivated to learn beyond grade-level expectations to accomplish the ambitious, real-world goals they set for themselves.

If we expect to help students meet rigorous academic expectations *and* develop the complex set of competencies they'll need for active participation in careers and citizenship, we need to cultivate and reinforce their engagement in learning throughout the K–12 years.

The following sections offer advice and strategies to put meaningful, real-world learning into action.

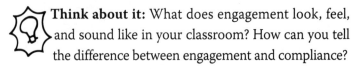 **Think about it:** What does engagement look, feel, and sound like in your classroom? How can you tell the difference between engagement and compliance?

Remember the Fourth *R*: Relevance

Nearly half of the students who took part in the High School Survey of Student Engagement (Yazzie-Mintz, 2010) said they were bored in school *every day*. Their top reasons: the material wasn't interesting (81.3 percent) and the material wasn't relevant *to me* (41.6 percent; emphasis added).

In contrast, students respond positively when teachers help them see the connection between what they are learning and the issues they face in their current lives, as well as what they will likely need to know in the future. Educational researcher Kristy Cooper (2014) calls this approach "connective instruction." She found this style of instruction to have the single biggest effect for increasing engagement—seven times the effect of other good practices, such as lively teaching and emphasis on academic rigor.

Another recent study on engagement in middle school underscores the importance of connecting learning with students' interests. Researchers (Wang & Eccles, 2013) found that students were more likely to express interest in and take ownership of their learning when they considered what they were studying to be personally interesting and relevant.

Although engagement is malleable, it doesn't increase simply by giving students more choices in learning activities; students need to see how those choices relate to their lives.

As Wang and Eccles (2013) explain, "Opportunities for decision making or freedom of action are less important than the extent to which the decision making and action opportunities available reflect personal goals, interests, or values" (p. 14).

Relevance doesn't mean projects have to be "all about me"; in fact, project experiences often have the emotional appeal of helping others. Witness an 8th grader's reflection on a project in which he used technology to improve life for a child with a physical handicap: "One of the bigger things I will take away from this is that, regardless of all the teachers saying, 'You can make a change,' and 'There are still plenty of opportunities to change the world,' that actually is true" (Boss, 2014a). Learning has emotional engagement when it conveys a sense of belonging and builds connections between students and their world (Yazzie-Mintz & McCormick, 2012).

The Connected Learning Research Network (http://clrn.dmlhub.net) reminds us that today's learners are eager for opportunities to collaborate with peers and experts, to pursue topics that are personally relevant, and to connect their academic studies to community issues. For a generation of young people who have grown up with ready access to digital information and the tools of production, learning isn't limited to what happens in the classroom or at the direction of the teacher.

The Alliance for Excellent Education report *Connected Learning: Harnessing the Information Age to Make Learning More Powerful* (Roc, 2014) suggests four ingredients for ensuring meaningful learning experiences:

1. Make learners the focus. This involves helping students become lifelong learners and develop the skills and knowledge they need to succeed in the 21st century.

2. Help students make the connection between their own interests and their academic studies and connect with inspiring mentors and peers to improve engagement.

3. Foster continuous learning. Continuous learning involves linking learning to school, home, and the community, so it can happen in any setting.

4. Help learners become makers and producers by teaching them to experiment, create, produce, and design.

For many students, relevance comes down to seeing the value of what they are learning, whether the value is in their own lives or in benefitting others. For example, English language learners at Tuttle Middle School collaborated with their public library to better serve the needs of adult Spanish speakers in their Indiana community. This was not a simple task. Students had to learn about their audience to understand their needs. To make the library collection more accessible, students translated book catalogs, wrote book reviews, and hosted a family open house. Students were motivated to improve their own language fluency, in both English and Spanish, so that they could help adults make better use of resources (Boss, 2013).

When projects are relevant, students understand why learning is worth the effort. They can see how others might benefit from their research or creativity. They feel motivated to put forward their best effort. These responses echo broader research on engagement, which shows that people who are engaged in their work are driven by four essential goals, each of which satisfies a particular human need (Strong, Silver, & Robinson, 1995): *success* (the need for mastery); *curiosity* (the need for understanding); *originality* (the need for self-expression); and *relationships* (the need for involvement with others).

Phil Schlechty (2011), a longtime advocate of student engagement, suggests watching for three signals that students are actively engaged in learning:

- They are attracted to their work.
- They persist in their work despite challenges and obstacles.
- They take visible delight in accomplishing their work.

 Think about it: Do you know what engages students outside the classroom? What do they create, produce, or design during their out-of-school time? How might you find out? (Hint: have students interview one another about their passions, interests, and talents.)

Find Project-Worthy Topics

As we have seen, real-world project ideas are all around us. Some projects start with teachers brainstorming to match their content standards to real-world context. They might ask, "How can we use statistics to predict our favorite athletes' performance in the Super Bowl, Olympic Games, World Cup, or other major sporting event?" "How does an understanding of geography help us imagine a healthier community?" or "How can the laws of physics help us design a more exciting (but safe) playground?"

Other projects begin with a student question, observation, interest, or concern that morphs into a full-blown project. For example, the wetlands restoration project described earlier started with a student asking, "Is there anything we can actually do to save an endangered species?"

I've even seen projects get under way because a community organization or other "client" enlisted students to help with problem solving. Imagine your students' response to these real requests: can you help us educate the public about how to recycle hazardous household waste? Can you help us design a zoo exhibit that will provide good habitat for its animal residents and be interesting to children who visit?

Let's take a closer look at some potential inspirations—and challenges—for designing real-world projects.

Rip Them from the Headlines

News events that generate a buzz of interest can spark compelling projects. In recent years, students across the United States have explored the environmental and social consequences of the massive *Deepwater Horizon* oil spill in the Gulf of Mexico; examined issues of race, politics, and identity after the election of the United States' first African American president; and developed disaster readiness plans for their own communities after watching Superstorm Sandy disrupt life and commerce for thousands of East Coast residents.

To become full-blown inquiry experiences, these "ripped-from-the-headlines" projects require deeper thinking than a quick class discussion of current events. The news event is merely the *hook*, or entry event, to launch an extended learning experience.

Projects that start with a news hook can be engaging but also present challenges. Teachers and students must dive deeply into topics for which there are no texts or guidebooks. They may need to think critically to determine which sources are trustworthy. Teachers need to be agile enough to respond to unfolding events that they can't predict. Maintaining student interest can be challenging once the headlines start to fade and media attention shifts to tomorrow's hot topic.

To evaluate whether a news story is project-worthy, first ask yourself if it concerns a messy problem. Does it involve a challenge for which there is no single correct answer? Students shouldn't be able to Google their way to a solution or find one in a textbook. Instead, arriving at a solution or response may require research, trial and error, and creativity. Effective problem solving may cut across disciplines and involve collaboration with partners who come at problems in different ways.

Breaking news may grab your students' attention, but will it sustain interest over time? Another clue to project worthiness: ask yourself if you can "teach backward" from a current event to engage students in an exploration of history. How can the past help us address or better understand a contemporary issue? How have we attempted to solve similar problems in previous eras?

This approach led Michigan social studies teacher Mike Kaechele to examine a headline-generating issue—rioting in Ferguson, Missouri, that erupted after the August 2014 fatal shooting of a young African American man—through a historical lens. To launch discussions, he created a graphic displaying side-by-side images of the Ferguson riots and the Boston Tea Party and posed the question "When is rioting justified?" In a blog post about how to navigate this kind of discussion with students, Kaechele (2014) encouraged teachers to invite students' questions as the first step into deeper inquiry. He also provided examples of questions that students might ask (perhaps with some artful teacher prompting), such as

- What are the similarities between the events?
- What are the differences?
- What are the issues that each side is upset about?
- Why is the image on the right called a "party"?
- The event on the right has been mythologized and treated as action by heroes. Do you think the event on the left will be?
- Should the people in either picture be considered heroes or criminals?

These are the kinds of questions that can lead students into deeper research, challenging them to arrive at their own interpretations of events both past and present. A similar approach can work in other disciplines as well. A STEM project involving innovation and design—for example, related to a news hook about alternative energy—might ask students to consider the question "How have people approached similar situations in the past, or in other parts of the world?"

What if your students feel far removed from an unfolding event? One strategy to make a topic more relevant is to connect students across distances. Collaboration enables those who live far from ground zero to "see" an issue through the eyes of peers who are experiencing it at close range. Teachers involved in the National Writing Project (NWP) have teamed up on several such collaborative projects, which build students' empathy and understanding of perspective along with communication skills. For examples of connected writing projects, visit the *Digital Is* website curated by the NWP (http://digitalis.nwp.org) or explore *Youth Voices*, a student publishing platform (http://youthvoices.net).

Ask the Experts

During projects, students often consult with content-area experts to test their ideas and gain practical feedback. Teachers would be wise to seek similar advice at the project design stage. By consulting with experts, you may be able to design more authentic projects while still incorporating the concepts you need to teach.

Leah Penniman, the science teacher quoted earlier, routinely consults with professional engineers when she is designing interdisciplinary math and science projects. She wants to know, *Is this the way engineers would approach a problem in the field?* She considers their advice while establishing project requirements but pays just as much attention to her own content standards and her students' mastery of concepts. Similarly, a journalism teacher might consult with a professional editor about issues relating to media ethics, or a physical education teacher might invite project feedback from a personal trainer or nutritionist.

Ensuring that projects are relevant and authentic as well as academically rigorous may feel like a tall order. It can be especially challenging for teachers who haven't worked in professions outside education. "Our teachers have had to figure out who in the 'real' world does things with the content I'm teaching? And how can I make it real-world without losing focus on what I'm responsible for teaching?" observes Todd Wigginton (quoted in Larmer, Mergendoller, & Boss, in press), coordinator of instructional projects for Metropolitan Nashville (TN) Public Schools.

To ensure authenticity in PBL, Nashville teachers sometimes have to investigate those connections themselves. "If teachers don't know who's using this content in the real world, we encourage them to seek out that information. Why are we teaching it? Why is it useful? Experts can help answer those questions," Wigginton adds. The district has established partnerships between schools and the local business and nonprofit community to facilitate those conversations.

Recruiting a project advisory team for your school offers another way to connect experts with the classroom, so that you don't have to start from scratch each time you want to consult. (Recruiting tips: look for content experts within your parent community, and seek support from school leadership in assembling an advisory team.) A teacher in a career-technical high school program near Atlanta, Georgia, whose students take on complex, interdisciplinary digital arts projects regularly checks in with his advisory team to make sure his students are using the same software and design tools that the pros use. That's another measure of project authenticity.

Enlist Student Input

Which issues do your students care about? What are their passions? Their answers can inspire projects with a high engagement factor. If you're not sure, start by asking students open-ended questions, such as

- What would you like to fix or improve in your community?
- What seems unfair in the world (or in your school or neighborhood)?
- What's a problem that you don't think adults are going to solve by the time you've grown up?

If students seem too reticent to share their passions aloud, consider conducting an online survey or using a brainstorming tool like Padlet (padlet.com) to ensure quieter voices are heard.

The resulting information should generate a list of potentially rich topics. Which ones involve problems that students might want to investigate further *and* that relate to content standards? That's the sweet spot for PBL. The standards question is usually left to teachers to answer, but it doesn't need to be. Some teachers personalize learning by inviting students to propose projects that address specific content standards or focus on areas in which they want to develop mastery. Goal setting is another factor for increasing student engagement.

Students who aren't used to having such a voice in their own education may need help identifying their passions. Help them think critically about potential problems close at hand. In the process, they will build background knowledge and get better at the fine art of "problem-finding," a foundation of design thinking (McIntosh, 2014). Let's say students suggest dissatisfaction with the school cafeteria—a topic that hits close to home. Getting students to clearly define the problem they seek to solve could lead them to bring up

- **Economic factors.** Does better food cost more? What's the real cost of the food we waste?
- **Nutrition.** If we offer more choices, will students pick more healthful foods?
- **Culture.** What do our favorite foods tell us about our family heritage? Why does lunch taste better when my grandma cooks it?
- **Behavior change.** How can we convince people to try new foods?
- **Sustainability.** Where does our food come from? Should school cafeterias support local farmers?

- **Business strategies.** What are the pros and cons of outsourcing food service to private contractors?

Before moving ahead with a project, students would need to home in on a driving question and define which problem they intend to solve. James Gemma's 5th grade class at Rhodes Elementary School in Cranston, Rhode Island, did just that for a social studies project that was part of Project Citizen, a national civics education program. The students narrowed their focus from cafeteria food in general to the quality of breakfast choices. Their final product was an advocacy campaign for a new school breakfast menu with less sugar. Their reasoning was backed by research and evidence, and they garnered support for their cause by taking the issue to the public via social media and a website about social change (Cowart, 2013).

Respond to Requests

Imagine your students' reaction to a community member or organization asking for their help to solve a problem. Authentic requests can be the starting point of highly meaningful, engaging projects. To justify using class time, you'll need to connect the request to learning goals, which may require some creativity on your part. But consider these real-world results from high schools in diverse contexts across the United States:

- Advanced math students help nonprofits analyze data and produce infographics to explain the impact of their work in the community.

- Students who are proficient at working with geographic information software produce detailed maps that help emergency responders navigate the unmarked roads in their rural community.
- In a technology-inspired approach to writing for authentic audiences, students teach visitors about important landmarks in their downtown with the use of QR codes that the tourists can scan on their smartphones.
- Creative teens produce music videos and a social media campaign to convince their peers not to drop out of high school.

These kinds of projects sometimes come about because an outside organization or partner recognizes that students are capable of serious work. By making projects public, students (and teachers) establish a reputation for excellence and build a brand for high-quality project work.

Find Right-Sized Challenges

A word of caution: sometimes students will want to take on issues that are just too massive or complex for PBL. Tackling an issue like global poverty can be overwhelming, and students are likely to come away from the experience feeling like they can't make a difference.

Instead, help students find their way to problems that are "right-sized": big enough to matter, small enough to tackle. For example, instead of focusing on illiteracy worldwide, consider the 4th graders' mobile lending library described above, created to encourage reading during the summer months. The students' solution was tightly focused on a specific question ("How can we improve our school's literacy rate?"), doable, and likely to produce real results.

That doesn't mean you should ignore bigger or more complex issues. For the 4th graders creating the mobile library, for example, it would be easy to make connections between literacy rates in their community and global education issues, such as those outlined in the United Nations Millennium Development Goals (www.un.org/millenniun goals). By focusing on a right-sized challenge close to home, students gain context to better understand bigger issues.

Think about it: Do you make an effort to bring media attention to your students' projects? For example, do you alert your district communications staff when you are planning a project showcase or other public event? The result goes beyond what one principal describes as "good news stories about education": there's also educational value in attracting attention. One PBL veteran makes a point of inviting local reporters to end-of-project events because their questions cause students to reflect on what they have learned in an authentic way.

Hook Interest Early (and Often)

Although your students' interests can be good starting places for projects, don't limit your focus to topics that students already know or care about. Meaningful learning experiences can ignite new interests and draw students into subjects they might not have found engaging in the past. The trick is hooking interest early and keeping students engaged across the arc of the project.

An engineering and technology project, for example, challenged a group of high school students to invent products or technology solutions that would make life easier for aging populations—people their grandparents' ages or older. To understand the needs of this user group, students first conducted interviews with seniors and observed residents at assisted living centers engaging in their daily activities. By getting to know their audience, they made an emotional connection to the task and were motivated to develop innovative solutions.

Similarly, a high school social studies project about conflicts in U.S. history began with students interviewing Vietnam War veterans in their small Northern California community. Many of the vets recalled their confusion of coming home amid antiwar protests. Hearing those first-person accounts—many never shared publicly before—got students thinking about their own responsibility as oral historians. Not only were they deeply engaged in exploring the politics of the Vietnam War era, but now they were also motivated to create an archive of veterans' stories and do justice to their experiences.

Hooking student interest early is important for project-based learning in general. A good entry event fires up curiosity and gets students asking questions. That's especially important for real-world projects that may take students outside their comfort zone or into unfamiliar territory.

Emphasize the real-world connections of a project right from the start by launching it with a shared experience that gets students interested, wondering, or emotionally connected. For example,

- Take students on a field trip that immerses them in the context you are investigating.
- Arrange a classroom visit (in person or via Skype or Google Hangout) from a guest speaker who has specific insights to share about a topic or an issue.
- Introduce a startling statistic or demonstration that challenges students' perceptions and makes them wonder, "How can this be true?"
- Share a provocative image or video clip.
- Issue a real request for help.

Any one of these activities should be enough to get students asking questions and feeling that they have a stake in finding answers. Entry experiences don't need to last long to be effective, but they should be genuine. That means steering clear of simulations or "fake real" events, as educator and author Sam Seidel cautions (Boss, 2012).

Maintain Engagement Through the Messy Middle

Once a project is off to a good start, continue to look for and encourage student engagement by making real-world connections. Throughout the project, keep the driving question front and center (for example, on your whiteboard, a project bulletin board, or a class wiki). This helps students make the connection between day-to-day learning activities and the overarching question they are aiming to answer. Whether students are analyzing a nonfiction text, producing multimedia products, taking part in a Socratic seminar, doing lab work, or conducting online research, they should see how each activity helps them go deeper into investigating and responding to the driving question.

If the project started with a news hook, use ongoing media coverage to keep students interested as they dig into their own research. For example, teachers may leverage students' interest in politics during a presidential election year as part of a social studies or an English language arts project. Take advantage of news coverage to keep students interested and thinking critically about media.

Another engagement tip: connect your students with others who are tackling similar issues. For example, you might set up a conversation with another class, elsewhere in the world, working on a similar project. Classes might connect virtually for a Skype conversation or Google Hangout, or they could post comments on each other's blogs. (See the Encore section for suggested resources to make online connections.)

Throughout the "messy middle" of the project, leverage formative assessment strategies to gauge student engagement as well as understanding. Use your powers of observation to determine if students are, in Phil Schlechty's (2011) words, "taking visible delight" in the learning experience. Use reflection prompts to find out whether they're willing to persist through challenges and setbacks.

As you check on student understanding (and adjust instruction accordingly), don't forget to ask whether students see the relevance of what they are learning. For example, students may get frustrated working with others on a group project. You may need to help them troubleshoot team dynamics and strengthen their collaborative skills. Make sure they understand that collaboration isn't just a school expectation; it's an essential skill for real-world success across a diverse array of careers.

The messy middle is also when students are fine-tuning their final products. Remind them that experts in numerous fields produce high-quality work through a process of rapid prototyping. They fail fast to find out what doesn't work and invite feedback to test their ideas at the rough-draft stage. Make sure students get frequent feedback and formative assessment, both strategies that make learning more effective (Hattie, 2012). Just as important, make sure the project calendar allows time for students to improve their work based on that feedback.

Students may need to be convinced that failing fast is in their best interest. Traditional schooling, after all, treats failure—the dreaded *F*—as the worst possible outcome of a learning experience. Share authentic examples of break-through ideas or products that came about through rapid prototyping, trial and error, or feeble first attempts. When you have opportunities for students to talk with experts from different disciplines, encourage them to describe the processes they use to produce worthy results.

Enlist Expert Support

In a previous section, we talked about the value of con-necting with experts at the project design stage to ensure authenticity. Content experts can play a valuable role in the middle of a project, too, by providing students with advice and critique.

Be creative with where you look for experts, and be specific in your requests for their time. You might consider the following questions:

- Who are the experts in dealing (or living) with the issue your students are investigating? How can you tap their perspective? These questions prompted students from Danette McMillian's financial literacy class to talk with their own family members about how to reduce household debt and improve their credit scores. Similarly, for a design project, high school students from Catlin Gabel School in Portland, Oregon, interviewed people about specific problems they experienced with footwear and then developed prototypes for shoes to cater to exactly this demographic. Students' designs were critiqued by design professionals from Oregon's athletic footwear industry.

- Who else is working to address this issue or topic? How can we engage with them or support their efforts? Take advantage of online communities and social media to make connections and exchange ideas with classrooms in other locations working on similar projects. Gifted education specialist Krissy Venosdale uses Twitter to share the questions her elementary students are trying to answer and often gets replies from experts willing to help.
- Which technology tools will help you make connections beyond the classroom? To connect across distances, take advantage of free videoconferencing tools such as Skype in the Classroom and Google Hangout.

Don't overlook peer (or near-peer) experts. Colleges are likely to have student associations of future engineers, scientists, educators, and entrepreneurs. High school art students can provide helpful critiques to elementary-level students working on illustrations for publishing projects.

As you are mapping out a project calendar, allow plenty of time for students to work through multiple drafts of their final products. This iterative process—learning from feedback, making improvements, reflecting on the experience—is how experts outside the classroom pursue excellence. Your students deserve the opportunity to "fail fast" and "fail forward" without being penalized for their learning process. Provide them with plenty of *ungraded* formative assessment and peer critique, and then allow time for them to make improvements based on feedback. The process will encourage persistence and risk taking—both important qualities for real-world success.

Think about it: Perhaps you're motivated to connect students with experts during the "messy middle" of projects. How will you prepare students to take advantage of this expertise and make good use of the limited time that professionals may have to offer?

From Talkers to Doers: Nudging Students Toward Action

Kelli Etheredge, a teacher at St. Paul's Episcopal School in Mobile, Alabama, admits that she sometimes has to give her students a gentle nudge to take their learning beyond the classroom. When her 10th graders published an online magazine as part of an environmental research project, the teacher says, "They thought they were done. I told them, 'You're not talkers—you're doers. What can we do about these issues in our community?'" (personal communication, July 1, 2014).

That prompted students to think about the river that flows through their hometown. "Every time it rains, the Dog River is full of trash. Then it all dumps into the bay," Etheredge says. "Students use this river all the time—they want it to be clean."

After thinking more critically about the causes and consequences of river pollution in their own hometown, students proposed replacing inefficient litter traps meant to keep debris out of the Dog River. To raise funds for their solution, they approached the owner of a local coffeehouse and asked if he would donate a portion of one day's profits. Once again, students found themselves on the defensive: "He told them, 'Doesn't sound like you're doing much work,'" Etheredge recalls. Instead of agreeing to a one-day donation, the owner challenged students to come up with a more marketable solution: a special blend of coffee to sell, branded with their logo and environmental message. All profits would go toward their cause. That was the inspiration for their Watershed Blend coffee.

When students take real action, they put lessons learned to authentic use. Engagement increases when students recognize opportunities to play an active part in their communities (Yazzie-Mintz & McCormick, 2012). This might mean local action, global activism, or a combination of the two. Think about projects that have "glocal" impact: raising students' awareness of global issues and trends while creating opportunities for them to make a difference locally. Think, too, about how you can help students avoid the too-easy approach of "slacktivism," or giving lip service to a cause without deeply engaging. Simply "liking" a cause on Facebook is not the same as taking meaningful action!

Think about it: How might you evaluate the success of projects that challenge students to take action? How can you help students think critically about where to focus their efforts for real impact? How are you ensuring that students have a voice and choice in action projects? Where might action-oriented projects lead?

Consider the Three As

When designing projects that have a service learning or citizenship focus, consider the three As: awareness, advocacy, and action. Any of these As can be a worthy outcome for a project. The challenge is to make sure it results from an authentic inquiry experience. Students can tell the difference between a project that gives them authentic voice and choice and a requirement to clock hours to meet a community service requirement.

Awareness. Awareness projects heighten students' understanding of an issue or a problem. Once students develop expertise or insights by exploring a topic in depth, they tend to be motivated to inform others about what they have learned.

Seventh grade students in Chicago, Illinois, responded to high gun violence rates in their community by raising awareness about individuals who strive to make their neighborhoods more peaceful. The project involved critical thinking and addressed important academic goals, such as persuasive writing, public speaking, and statistical analysis. Students developed their own criteria for the qualities that define a peacemaker. They conducted research to identify unsung heroes in their own neighborhoods and then interviewed these individuals to document their courageous stories. Students' awareness-raising efforts resulted in the publication of *Peacekeepers of Chicago*, an inspiring book filled with biographical essays and photo portraits (Polaris Charter Academy Class of 2014, 2013).

For an awareness project with a global focus, high school English students in Saskatchewan, Canada, took on the difficult issue of human trafficking. They were inspired to act by reading *Sold*, in which author Patricia McCormick addresses the difficult issue of modern slavery for young adult readers. To raise awareness of the issue and at the same time deepen their own digital literacy skills, they created a compelling social media campaign that included students "wearing" bar codes to raise awareness of human trafficking.

Advocacy. When students take on the role of advocates, they speak up for a cause or argue for a solution. A project involving advocacy challenges students to analyze issues from multiple perspectives, consider pros and cons, and make a convincing argument for their position. It's a chance for students to deepen and apply their critical thinking skills. Advocacy efforts drive students to apply the Common Core standards for argumentation and evidence and to communicate with an authentic purpose.

In Portland, Oregon, high school students lobbied their state legislature to remove toxins from the air. Their advocacy efforts were the result of an investigation into causes of poor air quality in the immediate neighborhood of their high school—rated one of the worst school sites in the country for exposure to toxins. The students' efforts engaged community members and built connections with research scientists. Students even traveled to Washington, D.C., to present their project at a national service learning conference.

Younger students, too, can find their voice as advocates. In Washington State, 7th graders lobbied for a bill to ban puppy mills, which produce large numbers of dogs that often wind up being sick or abandoned. Students presented a compelling case, backed by evidence and economic data.

On a smaller scale, students might advocate to change a school policy, such as blocking social media sites or prohibiting access to cell phones during the school day. To make their case, they might need to research how other schools have addressed the issue, consider counterarguments, and develop a suggested code of conduct for appropriate social media use—and consequences for violations.

Action. Action projects give students the opportunity to actually put their ideas to work—to be "doers, not talkers," as Kelli Etheredge says—and use their leadership and communication skills to get others on board.

At Realm Charter School in Berkeley, California, 8th graders have put their understanding of architecture and problem solving into action by designing, building, and stocking their own school library space. They also raised $78,000 on a crowdfunding site to buy materials and books. That's the kind of authentic result that teacher Emily Pilloton looks for in Studio H, described (www.projecthdesign.org/programs/studio-h) as "a design/build public school curriculum that sparks community development through real-world, built projects." The artifacts that students construct in the Studio H class not only enhance their community but also offer lasting reminders of what they have accomplished.

When given the opportunity and encouragement to act, students I have interviewed and watched in action have cleaned up public beaches, protected watersheds, improved bike safety, started e-waste recycling programs, helped older adults use technology, and much more. Challenge your students to be "doers, not talkers" by sharing examples of what other students have accomplished. Students who are interested in environmental action projects, for example, might be inspired by learning about winners of the Brower Youth Awards (www.broweryouthawards.org). And the National Youth Leadership Council (www.nylc.org) promotes service learning and showcases exemplary projects at its annual conference.

Think about it: How has your school approached community service in the past? How might service be different if it involved in-depth inquiry and student voice? How have you seen students respond when given a chance to make a difference?

Be Purposeful About Audience

At the end of a project, students typically share what they have learned or discovered with an audience. Depending on the project, students might publish their work online, make presentations at a public event, or pitch their ideas to a panel of judges. Once again, the more authentic the audience, the better.

According to veteran PBL teacher Don Wettrick, "Nothing is better than a project that gets community buy-in." He says connecting students with an authentic audience is key to driving engagement and helping students relate what they are learning to the real world: "My top two goals are to help students find great opportunities [for real-world problem solving], and then cheerlead them to a great audience" (quoted in Boss, 2014b).

Audience interactions might unfold on YouTube or Twitter, where Wettrick helps students navigate social media and build their digital brand. That's part of a 21st century skillset, too, for aspiring entrepreneurs. Face-to-face interactions are equally important. It's not unusual for Wettrick's high school students to make recommendations to the mayor of their Indiana community. Wettrick says, "There's no more authentic audience than the mayor when it comes to getting things done" (quoted in Boss, 2014b).

Students benefit from honest critique along with positive attention for their projects. "They don't need to hear, 'Good job!' They're better off when an expert tells them, 'That's not bad, but have you considered this, or you might want to look at that.' Oh, boy," Wettrick adds. "When a student gets that kind of response from an expert in a field, that's authentic" (quoted in Boss, 2014b).

To make these interactions as productive as possible, you may need to prepare audience members for the role they will play. By thinking more critically about audience interactions, you can make the most of this final phase of PBL. As you plan culminating events, consider the following three questions.

What do you want students to gain from the audience interaction?

- If it's technical feedback, think about inviting experts for a pitch session or judging panel.
- If it's response or action, think about having students make presentations to a community group or decision-making body (such as a school board, city council, or neighborhood association).

- If it's a celebration, think about inviting community members whose talents or contributions are being honored or recognized in student projects.

Who's the audience for the "real-world" version?

- If students are producing documentaries, plan a red-carpet screening event.
- If students are making sense of history, set up a museum-style exhibition.
- If students are producing literature, plan a book release party, author chat, or poetry slam.

How can technology connect students with wider audiences for greater impact? Some teachers use social media to share their students' work with a larger audience. Using the popular Twitter hashtag #comments4kids, for example, is a quick way to solicit comments for students' blog posts. Quadblogging.net is a free online platform for connecting student bloggers around the world and encouraging them to comment on one another's posts. Youthvoices. net is a curated online site for student publishing.

Creating a project website, publishing online books, or creating a class YouTube channel are more strategies to disseminate student work to a wide audience. English teacher George Mayo curated student work from an ambitious literature and architecture project based on *The Catcher in the Rye* on a website called *Constructing Holden Caulfield* (http://litarch.blogspot.com). Manor New Tech High School in Manor, Texas, hosts a YouTube channel to showcase videos made by both students and teachers (www.youtube.com/user/ManorNewTechHigh). And students from High Tech High in San Diego, California, have published books that are sold on Amazon.com, including a series of field guides to the urban ecosystem of San Diego Bay (e.g., *San Diego Bay: A Call for Conservation*).

If you're new to using social media for learning, take advantage of free tutorials and resources to help you think through online strategies for making connections. (See the Encore section for suggestions.)

 Think about it: Getting the right people in the room (or virtual space) for the culmination of a project is a great step. Make sure that the audience delivers more than applause (although that's important, too). How might you prepare audience members to take an active role in the event? For example, could you prepare them with sample questions, feedback forms, people's choice ballots, or other prompts?

Teacher Readiness: Consider Your Next Steps

Middle school science teacher Rich Lehrer was two decades into his career before he took the plunge into what he calls "real-life education." It took a combination of factors to convince Lehrer to tackle more authentic projects with his students. He remembers, a decade earlier, hearing a colleague at a conference talk about the environmental projects his students regularly did in their small town. "Whenever there's a need for environmental testing—soil or water—these high school students do it. I remember thinking, how amazing! But I wasn't ready yet to teach that way," Lehrer says (personal communication, May 1, 2014).

A turning point came when Lehrer and his students took a field trip to learn about the work of a humanitarian engineer named Amy Smith. At the Massachusetts Institute of Technology's D-Lab (Development through Dialogue, Design & Dissemination), Smith and colleagues use engineering, inexpensive technologies, and cross-cultural collaboration to design low-cost solutions for people in the developing world. Just a few examples: low-cost rainwater harvesting, waste collection cargo bicycles, and technologies that enable garbage pickers to create new products (and income) from trash.

"Seeing her inventions got me thinking about what a regular person could do. I started thinking of things my students could design or build. I'm not expecting them to come up with inventions to patent," Lehrer says, "but to educate them by putting them into contact with real things."

These days, his students at Brookwood School in Manchester, Massachusetts, learn about energy and engineering by designing clean-burning cookstoves for people in the developing world. They have built a prosthetic "Robohand," using open-source software and a 3D printer, for a 3-year-old boy with a birth defect. They collaborate with partners and experts around the globe, effectively removing the classroom walls so that they can engage with the world. "If anyone's thinking we can't do real things with kids," Lehrer says, "I'm telling you you're wrong" (Boss, 2014a).

Lehrer's story is a powerful reminder that readiness to try new teaching approaches can happen at any time during your career. It may begin with a small step or experience that gets you thinking about what students can do. Your motivation to explore real-world connections may come from students themselves, many of whom are becoming increasingly vocal about the kinds of learning experiences they want. (To tap into this network, follow the #stuvoice hashtag on Twitter.) Change may come about because of discussions with your colleagues, with parents and other stakeholders, or—best of all—with students themselves.

Chances are, your first forays into more real-world learning will raise new questions. Give yourself the same permission that you give to students to improve your work with feedback, multiple drafts, and comments from trusted advisors. As you find your comfort zone as project designer and facilitator, you'll be modeling for students what it means to be a curious, active learner who engages with the world.

Think about it: Envision a project that not only engages students with the world and deepens their understanding but also builds their confidence as problem solvers and advocates for the future they imagine. What are you willing to change about your current teaching practices to make this happen? Which aspects of your teaching do you want to stay the same? Where in the world might your next project take you?

To give your feedback on this publication and
be entered into a drawing for a free ASCD
Arias e-book, please visit
www.ascd.org/ariasfeedback

ASCD | arias™

ENCORE

PROJECT-BASED LEARNING RESOURCES

The following resources will help you learn more about planning, managing, and assessing project-based learning.

Books

- *PBL for 21st Century Success: Teaching Critical Thinking, Collaboration, Communication, and Creativity* by Suzie Boss. (2013). Novato, CA: Buck Institute for Education.
- *PBL Starter Kit* by John Larmer, David Ross, and John R. Mergendoller. (2009). Novato, CA: Buck Institute for Education.
- *Reinventing Project-Based Learning: Your Field Guide to Real-World Projects in the Digital Age (2nd ed.)* by Suzie Boss and Jane Krauss. (2014). Eugene, OR: International Society for Technology in Education.
- *Teaching the iGeneration: Five Easy Ways to Introduce Essential Skills with Web 2.0 Tools* by William M. Ferriter and Adam Garry. (2010). Bloomington, IN: Solution Tree.
- *Thinking Through Project-Based Learning: Guiding Deeper Inquiry* by Jane Krauss and Suzie Boss. (2013). Thousand Oaks, CA: Corwin.

Online Resources

- **Buck Institute for Education** (www.bie.org): BIE promotes PBL to improve 21st century teaching and learning. The nonprofit organization maintains an extensive online library of sample project plans and videos and offers downloadable tools for project planning, management, and assessment.
- **Edutopia** (www.edutopia.org): Produced by the George Lucas Educational Foundation, Edutopia promotes PBL as a key strategy to improve teaching and learning. The website includes an extensive library of videos, articles, blogs, research summaries, classroom guides, and online communities where educators can connect and seek advice.
- **PBLU** (www.pblu.org): A project of the Buck Institute for Education, PBLU offers online classes in the basics of PBL. In addition, detailed project plans are available to download and adapt to your classroom context.

Connected Learning Resources

A number of resources are available to connect educators who share similar instructional goals and to connect your students with other learners around the world.

- **Comments4Kids** (http://comments4kids.blogspot.com): Using the Twitter hashtag #comments4kids, teachers can solicit comments for student blogs and other online publications. An accompanying website showcases project examples and shares teacher strategies for digital learning.

- **ePals** (www.epals.com): The ePals Global Community is a collaborative space for sharing project ideas and connecting classrooms for global learning experiences.
- **iEARN** (www.iearn.org): iEARN, the International Education and Resource Network, connects teachers and students to collaborate on projects that make a positive difference in the world.
- **The Global Classroom Project** (http://theglobalclassroomproject.wordpress.com): This online community has become a network for developing collaborative global projects and sharing effective teaching strategies for connected learning.
- **Quadblogging** (http://quadblogging.com): A platform to encourage authentic audiences for student writers, Quadblogging connects four classrooms, from anywhere in the world, to serve as one another's blog commenters.
- **Skype in the Classroom** (https://education.skype.com): This an online platform for connecting with other classrooms, engaging with experts, and taking virtual field trips, all using Skype for videoconferencing.

Social Media Resources

- **Facebook for Educators and Community Leaders** (http://fbhost.promotw.com/fbpages/img/safety_ resources/ffeclg.pdf): Published by Facebook, this downloadable guide discusses a range of topical issues, including digital citizenship, bullying prevention, and how to develop social media guidelines for schools.
- **The Teacher's Guide to Twitter** (www.edudemic. com/guides/guide-to-twitter): Published by Edudemic, this online guide explains the basics of how to use Twitter in the classroom and how to use it to connect with professional colleagues online.
- **The Teacher's Guide to Using YouTube in the Classroom** (www.edudemic.com/youtube-in-classroom): Published by Edudemic, this brief introduction covers the basics of using YouTube for education.

Talk It Over: Questions for Discussion

If you are planning to discuss this publication with your professional learning community or other study group, here are some questions to spark collegial conversations.

1. Relevance. Opportunities to emphasize the relevance of learning experiences come up across the arc of projects. Discuss your strategies for encouraging authenticity and real-world connections when you are

- *Designing projects:* How do you ensure that projects connect to students' interests *and* address content standards? How do you learn about students' interests?
- *Launching projects:* What have you planned as a hook for capturing student interest at the outset? How do you make sure projects remain engaging throughout the "messy middle"?
- *Connecting with experts:* How have you engaged experts to offer advice or critique of student work? How have students responded to advice from content experts?
- *Sharing projects:* Who is the audience most likely to care about the work that your students have produced? How will you recruit an authentic audience and prepare the audience to offer constructive feedback?

2. Engagement. Think about Phil Schlechty's (2011) three indicators of engagement (students are attracted to their work; they persist despite challenges and obstacles; they take visible delight in accomplishing their work). When have you seen a similar response from your students? What was the task or project that led to engagement? How do you define *engagement*? What's the evidence that tells you students are invested in learning?

3. Planning for action. Talk about the three *A*s described above (awareness, advocacy, and action) as possible project outcomes. Have you experienced similar outcomes with your students in the past? If so, what was the result? How do you think students would respond to the three *A*s as project goals? What might be potential challenges of asking students to be "doers, not talkers"? Do you see opportunities to combine global themes with local action (sometimes called "glocal" learning)?

4. Next steps. What are your next steps for putting the ideas presented here into action? If you are part of a PLC or other study group, how might you support one another as you move forward with real-world learning?

References

Amos, J. (2008). *Dropouts, diplomas, and dollars: U.S. high schools and the nation's economy.* Washington, DC: Alliance for Excellent Education. Retrieved from http://all4ed.org/reports-factsheets/dropouts-diplomas-and-dollars-u-s-high-schools-and-the-nations-economy

Boss, S. (2012, June 20). For engaging projects, "keep it real" [blog post]. Retrieved from *Edutopia* at http://www.edutopia.org/blog/pbl-world-conference-part-three-suzie-boss

Boss, S. (2013). *PBL for 21st century success: Teaching critical thinking, collaboration, communication, and creativity.* Novato, CA: Buck Institute for Education.

Boss, S. (2014a, June 10). Innovative education: Make room for "what-ifs" [blog post]. Retrieved from *Edutopia* at http://www.edutopia.org/blog/innovative-ed-what-if-thinking-making-room-suzie-boss

Boss, S. (2014b, February 21). Focus on audience for better PBL results [blog post]. Retrieved from *Edutopia* at http://www.edutopia.org/blog/focus-on-audience-for-better-pbl-results-suzie-boss

Cooper, K. S. (2014, April). Eliciting engagement in the high school classroom: A mixed-methods examination of teaching practices. *American Educational Research Journal, 51,* 363–402.

Costa, A. L., & Kallick, B. (2008). *Learning and leading with habits of mind: 16 essential characteristics for success.* Alexandria, VA: ASCD.

Cowart, J. (2013, June 5). Project Citizen students want better school breakfasts. *Cranston Online.* Retrieved from http://cranstononline.com/stories/Project-Citizen-students-want-better-school-breakfasts,82689?print=1

Gallup, Inc. (2013). *2013 Gallup student poll results.* Retrieved from http://www.gallupstudentpoll.com/174020/2013-gallup-student-poll-overall-report.aspx

Hattie, J. (2012). *Visible learning for teachers: Maximizing impact on learning.* New York: Routledge.

Kaechele, M. (2014, August 18). Ferguson vs. Boston [blog post]. Retrieved from *Concrete Classroom* at http://www.michaelkaechele.com/ferguson-vs-boston

Klem, A. M., & Connell, J. (2004, September). Relationships matter: Linking teacher support to student engagement and achievement. *Journal of School Health, 74*(7), 262–273.

Larmer, J., & Mergendoller, J. R. (2010). *The main course, not dessert: How are students reaching 21st century goals? With 21st century project based learning.* Novato, CA: Buck Institute for Education.

Larmer, J., Mergendoller, J. R., & Boss, S. (in press). *Setting the Standard for Project-Based Learning: A Proven Approach to Rigorous Classroom Instruction.* Alexandria, VA: ASCD.

McIntosh, E. (2014). *How to come up with great ideas and actually make them happen.* Edinburgh, UK: NoTosh Publishing.

Miller, K., Vaughan, R., & Worthy, J. (Presenters). (2014, July 17). EAST at Sonora Elementary presents at Esri conference [Video]. Retrieved from http://www.eastinitiative.org/newsopportunities/NewsStory.aspx?Id=1446

Penniman, L. (2014, April 1). Real-world learning: Applying science in global service [blog post]. Retrieved from *Tchers' Voice* at http://www.teachingchannel.org/blog/2014/04/01/deeper-learning-science-in-global-service

Polaris Charter Academy Class of 2014. (2013). *Peacekeepers of Chicago.* Retrieved from http://elschools.org/student-work/peacekeepers-chicago

Roc, M. (2014). *Connected learning: Harnessing the information age to make learning more powerful.* Washington, DC: Alliance for Excellent Education. Retrieved from http://all4ed.org/wp-content/uploads/w/03/ConnectedLearning.pdf

Schlechty, P. C. (2011). *Engaging students: The next level of working on the work.* San Francisco: Jossey-Bass.

Strong, R., Silver, H. F., & Robinson, A. (1995, September). Strengthening student engagement: What do students want (and what really motivates them)? *Educational Leadership, 53*(1), 8–12.

Thomas, J. W. (2000, March). *A review of research on project-based learning.* San Rafael, CA: The Autodesk Foundation. Retrieved from http://www.bobpearlman.org/BestPractices/PBL_Research.pdf

Wang, M., & Eccles, J. S. (2013). School context, achievement motivation, and academic engagement: A longitudinal study of school engagement using a multidimensional perspective. *Learning and Instruction, 28,* 12–23.

White, K., & Donnenfield, D. (Producers, Writers, and Directors). (2009). *A simple question: The story of STRAW* [Film]. San Francisco: Filmmakers Collaborative SF.

Yazzie-Mintz, E. (2010). *Charting the path from engagement to achievement: A report on the 2009 High School Survey of Student Engagement.* Bloomington, IN: Center for Evaluation & Education Policy. Retrieved from http://ceep.indiana.edu/hssse/images/HSSSE_2010_Report.pdf

Yazzie-Mintz, E., & McCormick, K. (2012). Finding the humanity in the data: Understanding, measuring, and strengthening student engagement. In S. L. Christenson, A. L. Reschly, & C. Wylie (Eds.), *Handbook of research on student engagement* (pp. 743–762). New York: Springer.

Zhao, Y. (2012, August 16). Doublethink: The creativity-testing conflict [blog post]. Retrieved from *Zhao Learning* at http://zhaolearning.com/2012/08/16/doublethink-the-creativity-testing-conflict

Related Resources

At the time of publication, the following ASCD resources were available (ASCD stock numbers appear in parentheses). For up-to-date information about ASCD resources, go to www.ascd.org. You can search the complete archives of *Educational Leadership* at http://www.ascd.org/el.

ASCD EDge®
Exchange ideas and connect with other educators interested in project-based learning on the social networking site ASCD EDge at edge.ascd.org.

Print Products
Authentic Learning in the Digital Age: Engaging Students Through Inquiry by Larissa Pahomov (#115009)
Engineering Essentials for STEM Instruction: How do I infuse real-world problem solving into science, technology, and math? by Pamela Truesdell (#SF114048)
Great Performances: Creating Classroom-Based Assessment Tasks (2nd ed.) by Larry Lewin and Betty Jean Shoemaker (#110038)
Role Reversal: Achieving Uncommonly Excellent Results in the Student-Centered Classroom by Mark Barnes (#113004)

DVDs
21st Century Skills: Promoting Creativity and Innovation in the Classroom (#609096)
The Innovators: Project Based Learning and the 21st Century (#613043)

ASCD PD Online® Course
Project-Based Learning: An Answer to the Common Core Challenge (#PD13OC008M)

For more information: send e-mail to member@ascd.org; call 1-800-933-2723 or 703-578-9600, press 2; send a fax to 703-575-5400; or write to Information Services, ASCD, 1703 N. Beauregard St., Alexandria, VA 22311-1714 USA.

About the Author

Suzie Boss is a writer and educational consultant who focuses on the power of teaching and learning to improve lives and transform communities. She is the author or coauthor of four books on education, including *Bringing Innovation to School: Empowering Students to Thrive in a Changing World* and *Thinking Through Project-Based Learning: Guiding Deeper Inquiry.* She is a regular contributor to *Edutopia* and the *Stanford Social Innovation Review,* and a member of the Buck Institute for Education National Faculty. Her work has appeared in a wide range of publications, including *Educational Leadership, Principal Leadership,* the *New York Times, Education Week,* and the *Huffington Post.*

She is a frequent presenter at conferences and consults internationally with schools interested in shifting from traditional instruction to technology-rich, project-based learning. Inspired by educators who push the boundaries of the traditional classroom, she also has developed informal learning programs that teach youth and adults how to improve their communities with innovative, sustainable solutions. Her wide-ranging interests in education were shaped by her work as a writer, an editor, and a field researcher for the Northwest Regional Educational Laboratory (now called Education

Northwest) in Portland, Oregon. She can be reached at suzieboss@gmail.com.

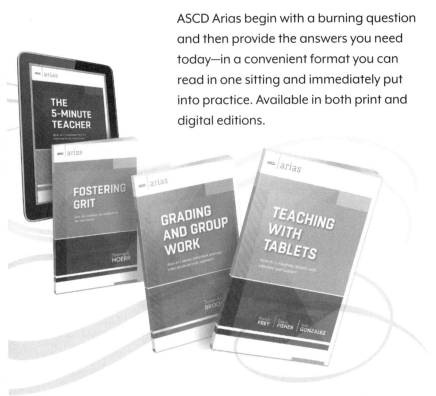